LIVE
CHILLERS

E-mail

Barbara Mitchelhill

Published in association with
The Basic Skills Agency

Hodder & Stoughton

A MEMBER OF THE HODDER HEADLINE GROUP

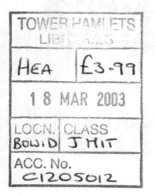

Acknowledgements
Cover: Stuart Williams
Illustrations: Jim Eldridge

Orders; please contact Bookpoint Ltd, 39 Milton Park, Abingdon, Oxon OX14
4TD. Telephone: (44) 01235 400414, Fax: (44) 01235 400454. Lines are open
from 9.00–6.00, Monday to Saturday, with a 24 hour message answering service.
Email address: orders@bookpoint.co.uk

British Library Cataloguing in Publication Data
A catalogue record for this title is available from the British Library

ISBN 0 340 77602 1

First published 2000
Impression number 10 9 8 7 6 5 4 3 2 1
Year   2005 2004 2003 2002 2001 2000

Typeset by GreenGate Publishing Services, Tonbridge, Kent.
Printed in Great Britain for Hodder and Stoughton Educational, a division of
Hodder Headline Plc, 338 Euston Road, London NW1 3BH, by Atheneum
Press, Gateshead, Tyne & Wear

E-mail

Contents

1

Walker and Greenly

Kenny had always loved the night time –
he was a real night owl.
Sometimes, it got him into trouble.
Like two years ago when he broke into a shop.
It was just a laugh.
Something to do after the pubs had shut.
All the same, he did time for it.
But that was behind him now.
He was going straight.
He'd moved to a new town and found a job.
Nobody knew about his past. He'd lied.

He liked his job a lot. He worked on
night security at Walker and Greenly.
They were a large firm of accountants,
with pots of money.
The offices were on the top three floors
of Melkon Towers.
Right in the middle of the city.

Kenny started at eight every evening.
Some of the time he watched TV monitors
in the control room.
There were security cameras all over the place.
There were twenty monitors to watch.
He had to check the office doors,
as well as the alarm system.

There were two security guards –
Kenny and Tosh.
They always worked together.
One night when Tosh was off sick,
Kenny was left on his own.
That's when things started to go wrong.

He had finished checking the offices.
Everything was OK.
It was then he did a stupid thing.
He had always fancied trying out the computer.
Now was his chance.
He could leave the monitors
to look after themselves for five minutes.
Nobody would know.

Kenny had a mate called Dean
who lived in the same block of flats.
Dean was mad about computers.
He had one of his own.
He'd shown Kenny how to use it.
Dean could surf the Internet and send e-mails.
He was really clever with computers.

'No reason why I can't do it,' Kenny said
as he sat in the receptionist's chair.
'I'll send an e-mail to Dean.
It'll be a laugh.'
He leaned across the desk
and switched the computer on.

The screen flickered into life
and Kenny put his fingers on the keys.
He tapped his way into the Internet.
He waited until he saw a small envelope
on the screen. Underneath it, it said 'e-mail'.

'Yes!' he said under his breath.
But before he could click the mouse button,
he heard something ... He turned and listened.
He could hear footsteps!
Someone was moving around on the floor
above.

2

Brenda

Kenny reached over and flicked the switch.
The screen died and turned black.
Then he slid off the chair and
crouched under the desk, listening.
The footsteps were coming nearer.
They were on the stairs.
How had somebody got past the alarm?
The building was wired from top to bottom.
His heart was pounding in his chest.
His head was full of terrible thoughts.
He might get beaten up.

Even if he stayed out of sight,
he'd still lose his job.
Old Rawlins would say
he should have been watching the monitors.
Whatever happened, he was for it.

He looked up and saw the camera fixed
to the ceiling. He smiled.
The intruders wouldn't see it.
But everything they did would be on film
and they'd be nicked!
The footsteps came nearer ... and nearer ...
He held his head in his hands ...
and then he heard singing!
He couldn't believe it! He looked up.

'Brenda!' he said. 'What are you doing here?
The cleaners went home hours ago.'
'Oh hello, Kenny, love!' she said.
'I've been doing extra.
Mr Bolt wanted me to do his office
before I start my hols.
Don't think he trusts the other cleaners.'

She leaned forward,
tapped her nose and winked.
'He always leaves such a lot of papers
on his desk, see.'
She laughed. 'Anyway, I'm off.
Pass me my bag will you.
Sharon lets me keep it in that bottom drawer.'

Kenny grinned and opened the filing cabinet.
'Frightened one of the others
might nick your money, Brenda?'

'Course not!' she said. 'Give it here. I'm off.
And I won't see you for a fortnight.
I'm off to the Costa Brava!'
'Don't do anything I wouldn't!' said Kenny.
'I shan't!' she said with a laugh.
And with that, she put her bag
on her shoulder and headed for the lift.

So it was only Brenda, after all!
Kenny breathed a sigh of relief and sat down.
He could still send the e-mail.
He was about to turn on the computer,
when he remembered the security camera.
'I don't want you spying on me,' he said,
looking up at the secret eye.
'I'll switch you off for a bit.
That way Old Rawlins won't see what I'm up to
if he does a check.'
So Kenny went up to the control room
and switched off the camera.
That was mistake number one.
His biggest mistake was yet to come.

3

Kenny's Mistake

In less than five minutes,
Kenny was back in the lobby,
sitting at the desk.
'Now to access the Internet,' he muttered.
He pressed the switch and the screen lit up.
He clicked on the mouse and paused until
the small envelope appeared on the screen.
He clicked again and began to type.

Hi Dean! I'm down in reception
at Walker and Greenly
instead of sitting in front of the monitors.
This computer's dead easy.
Tosh is off sick so there's only me
looking after all the offices.
What if somebody breaks in
while I'm doing this?
Will you pay my bail if I get put in the nick?
Send me an e-mail now, if you're still awake.
From Kenny Web.

Dean often messed about with his computer
late at night.
There was a good chance he'd see the e-mail.

Kenny tried to remember the e-mail address.
It's d for Dean, e for Eric and w for William.
Then his last name – Links.
Then @aol.com.
Brilliant! Yeah! That's it.

He quickly tapped it out,
but he was not careful enough. He typed:
newlinks@aol.com
Ooops! That's wrong he thought.
How do I change the n for a d?
He pressed the delete button
but nothing happened.
He tried again but it stayed the same.
He'd have to start on a new line
and type Dean's e-mail address again.
He pressed each key slowly,
making sure there were no mistakes.
dewlinks@aol.com
'Gotcha!' he said and pressed SEND.

The machine bleeped. The writing disappeared
and a swirling pattern filled the screen.
The e-mail had gone.
Kenny decided to give Dean twenty minutes.
If he hadn't replied by then,
he'd shut the computer down.
He went off to check the monitors
and make a cup of coffee.

When he came back,
there was a message on the screen.
YOU HAVE E-MAIL.
Kenny clicked on the mouse.
What had Dean written? he wondered.
He watched as the text flickered
onto the screen.
But he was in for a surprise.
Dean hadn't sent the reply.
It had come from New Links Corporation.
And that was when the serious trouble began.

4

The Choice

Kenny leaned forward and read the message.
New Links Corporation knows who you are.
You are a liar and a thief.
We could tell Walker and Greenly
you are tapping into the office computer.
They'll go to the police and find out you've
got a record. They'll find out you lied.
Lucky for you we won't ring the company –
so long as you do something for New Links.
Send a reply at once.

He stared at the screen. It was a joke, right?
Somebody wanted to spook him.
But who knew he'd been inside?
Even Dean didn't know that. Kenny felt sick.
He felt he should take this seriously.
He put his hands on the keyboard
and tapped out a message.
What is New Links and what do you want?
He pressed SEND and it disappeared
off the screen.

He sat there waiting.
He knew he ought to be back
in the control room.
He should be watching the monitors.
That was what he was paid for after all.
He'd wait five minutes and then he'd go.

In less than two, the message came:
YOU HAVE E-MAIL.
It was the answer to his question.

New Links is the brains behind
computer dealing.
We take from the big companies
and give to the poor.
We are the poor! Ha ha!
You are our latest recruit.
This is what we want you to do:
Go to the Managing Director's office.
One of his clients is Stikton International.
Find the file and let us have the banking code.
Not only will you keep your job –
you'll take a share of the profits.
What have you got to lose?
Remember! If you don't come in on the deal,
we ring your company.
The choice is yours.
We give you half an hour.

Kenny thought hard.
What choice did he have?
Do as they say or refuse and lose his job.
Slowly, he got up and walked out of reception.

He went down the corridor to the control room.
The keys were in the cupboard on the wall.
With a shaking hand, he tapped in the code.
The lock sprang open revealing the keys
to every room in the building.
Kenny took a deep breath
and then grabbed the bunch marked
Mr C Bolt, Managing Director – office no. 4.

Kenny's part in a massive computer theft
had begun.

5

The Deed is Done

As Kenny stood in the doorway
of Mr Bolts office, he felt sick.
What was he doing here? He should leave.
Ring the Police. But he daren't.
He had too much to lose.
He looked around the room.
Brenda was right about the desk.
It was a real mess and was covered in papers.
At one end he saw there was a stack of files.
Kenny walked quickly over to the desk.
He searched through the pile carefully.

Then, right near the bottom, he found it –
the file on Stikton International.

This was it! His hand grasped the file.
His brain knew it was wrong
but still he held it.

As he walked towards the reception desk,
the computer screen blinked at him.
He put the file down and opened it
to find the banking code.
Then he tapped the code onto the screen
and pressed SEND.

He had done it.
He had given away the secret code.
Stikton's bank account would be wide open
to any crook.
Their money could be transferred
to another account in minutes.
His head began to swim
as the message vanished from the screen.
He groaned and his head slumped onto
the desk.

6

On Film

Kenny lifted his head slowly.
He felt bad and his mouth was dry.
How could he have fallen asleep?
Wasn't he in enough trouble already?
He squinted and looked down at his watch.
Five thirty! He'd been out for hours.
Then he noticed the file next to the computer.
His pulse began to race.
He had to put it back. Nobody must find out.
He would give in his notice.
Move to a new town. Change his name.

He stood up and stuffed the file under his arm.
He ran up the stairs two at a time,
pulling out his keys as he went.
By the time he arrived at office number 4,
he was gasping for breath.
His hands were shaking so much that it
was difficult to push the key in the keyhole.
'Go in you devil!' he shouted.
'Come on! Give me a break!'

At last the key turned
and he pushed the door open.
He looked at Mr Bolt's desk.
Where exactly had the file been?
He tried to calm down and think clearly.
But he couldn't remember.
In the end, he put it on the top of the pile.
That looked OK. He closed his eyes and said,
'Please let it be right.
Don't let them find out I moved them.'
He turned quickly and walked to the door.
As he did so, he noticed the camera.
Security camera 4!

Of course! It would all be on film.
It would show him taking the file and
returning it.
He slammed the office door and locked it.
Then he raced back down the stairs ...
through the lobby and into the control room.

Every camera had a different cassette.
There were cassettes for each day
of the week.
It was Kenny's job to put new films in
when he started his shift.

He went to the cupboard where they were kept
and took one from the shelf marked 'camera 4'.
'This is yesterday's cassette,'
he said to himself. 'I'll swap it.
Nobody will know. Nobody will check.'
He removed the tell-tale cassette from the
machine and replaced it with the old one.
All he had to do now
was to wipe the film clean.
There was a special machine he could use.

But he never did use it.
As he stood with the cassette in his hand,
he heard the hum of the lift …
the clunk as it stopped at the thirteenth floor …
then footsteps in the lobby.

Kenny looked at his watch. It was six o'clock.
He knew who it was.
It was Old Rawlins, his supervisor,
and he would come straight to the control room.
He would catch him red handed.

7

Another Message

Kenny stuffed the cassette up his sweatshirt.
'Everything all right?' asked Rawlins.
Kenny nodded and swung round
to face his boss.
He looked as though he'd been there for hours.
'Quiet night,' he said. 'Brenda left late.
She'd been cleaning Mr Bolt's office.
Nothing else to report.'
Rawlins glanced at the monitors.
'Why is camera 1 out?' he said.
'The screen's blank or hadn't you noticed?'
He stepped towards the control panel.

23

Kenny panicked as he remembered.
He'd switched it off when he was messing
with the computer in the lobby.
'Er … the switch might be faulty,' he said,
leaning forward and flicking it on.
The monitor lit up immediately.
'How long has it been like that?'
barked Rawlins. 'Why didn't you report it?'
'It seems all right now,' said Kenny.

Rawlins didn't seem convinced.
'I'd better check the offices,' he said.
He marched towards the stairs
and Kenny hurried after him,
clutching the cassette against his stomach.
He could tell that Rawlins was angry.
After checking all the office doors,
Kenny walked with him to the lobby.
Then he let out a silent gasp of horror.
The computer on the reception desk!
He had forgotten to switch it off!
Would Rawlins notice it?
Maybe not.

Suddenly Rawlins stopped. 'What on earth …'
Kenny turned to his boss,
hardly daring to look.
But Rawlins was pointing beyond the desk.
'An empty cigarette packet!' he bellowed.
'This place is a pigsty. I'll have a word
with the cleaning staff tomorrow.'
With that, Rawlins marched towards the lift
without even saying goodbye.

Once he'd gone, Kenny pulled the cassette out
from under his sweatshirt.
Now he could go back and wipe it clean.
Clear away the evidence.
But first he must switch the computer off.

He walked behind the desk to turn it off.
Then he saw the message on the screen.
E-MAIL WAITING.
An icy chill ran down his spine.
He knew he should switch the machine off.
But he had to know what the e-mail said.
He had to know …

8

Visitors

Kenny read the words on the screen.
THANKS SUCKER!
NOW WE'LL WIPE YOU OFF OUR
EMPLOYMENT LIST!
He should have known.
They had no intention of sharing the money.
The only thing he could do
was to get rid of the evidence.
He had to wipe the video tape clean
for one thing.
He'd have to hurry. In an hour or so,
everyone would be coming to work.
He leaned forward to switch off the machine.

Then he realised the e-mails were still on
the computer file. Anyone could access them.
He didn't know how to delete them.
He played around. Clicking on the mouse.
Using the delete key. It was useless.
He tried again until his temper snapped.
'NO!' he yelled.
'YOU WON'T GET THE BETTER OF ME!'
He raised his fist ready to smash the machine.

'KENNY! WHAT ARE YOU DOING?'
Brenda's voice came from behind him.
'Brenda! What are you doing here?
I thought you were going to Spain.'
'I am,' she said. 'There's a taxi outside
waiting to take me to the airport.'
'Then why ...?'
'My passport must have dropped out of my bag,'
she said. 'But what on earth are you up to?'

There didn't seem any point in keeping it
to himself. Kenny told her everything ...
He told her about the e-mails
and the file and the transfer of the money.

'I've never heard anything like it!' she said.

'We need the police, my lad.

You won't do any good by telling more lies.

We might even be in time to get the money back.

You ring 999 and I'll go down to cancel the taxi.'

'But ...'

'Don't argue, Kenny,' she said.

'New Links Corporation sounds very dangerous.'

She stood by the lift and pressed the button.

'Funny,' she said.

'The lift's gone down to the ground floor.'

She pressed the button again to make sure.

They heard the hum of the lift
as it rose to the thirteenth floor.
They heard the clunk as it stopped.
They heard the swish as the doors slid open.

Two men stepped out. They were thick set
with dark hair cropped closed to the skull.
'You must be expecting us,' one said.
'We're from New Links Corporation.'